Date With Disaster!

Claire Powell

LEVEL 1

SCHOLASTIC

Material written by: Claire Powell

Commissioning Editor: Jacquie Bloese

Editor: Fiona Beddall

Cover design: Ian Butterworth, Emily Spencer

Designer: Dawn Wilson

Illustrator: Susannah Fishburne

Picture research: Emma Bree

Photo credits: Cover: A. Pollok/Taxi/Getty Images; Rubberball; Stockdisc. **Pages 4 & 5:** Pollok/Taxi/Getty Images; Rubberball; Stockdisc; R. Stainforth/Alamy; Brand X. **Page 28:** Image100. **Pages 24 & 25:** Stockbyte; Imagesource; Hemera; S. Botterill/Getty Images; S. Bond/Alamy.

The publishers would like to acknowledge the following teachers for reporting on the manuscript:

Carine Chaput, Collège Ozar Hatorah, Toulouse, France

Kleio Drosou, Vytina High School, Arcadia, Greece

Beata Eigner, GRG, Vienna, Austria

Marie-Christine Jacquot, Collège Saint-Maimboeuf, Montbeliard, France

Adele James, Nea Paideia, Hydrari, Greece

Brigitte Neustifter, SHS Weiz, Weiz, Austria

Gertraud Noeth, Christian-von-Bomhard Schule, Uffenheim, Germany

Theodora Papavasiliou, English Language Centre, Trikala, Greece

Monique Peubez, Institution des Chartreux, Lyon, France

Maria Santoliquido, IPSCP 'Marcello Dudovich', Milan, Italy

Mary Glasgow Magazines (Scholastic Ltd.)
Euston House
24 Eversholt Street
London NW1 1DB

Printed in Singapore. Reprinted in 2009.

Contents

Date With Disaster!

KATE

How old? 13
Lives: in Aylesbury, with her mum, dad and sister Rachel
Favourite music: Kelis, Usher, Beyoncé, Jamelia, Joss Stone
Likes: singing, reading magazines, watching films
Wants to be: a famous singer

JOE

How old? 14
Lives: in Aylesbury, with his mum, dad and two brothers
Favourite music: everything from 50 Cent to Maroon 5
Likes: music, football, going to clubs, new friends
Wants to be: in a famous band, or maybe a DJ

IAN

How old? 13
Lives: in Aylesbury, with his mum and dad
Favourite music: Robbie Williams, Dido
Likes: maths, going to the cinema, playing football
Wants to be: good at lots of different things

RACHEL

How old? 18
Lives: in Brighton, and with her family in Aylesbury in the holidays
Favourite music: Alicia Keys, Blue, Maroon 5
Likes: shopping, going to clubs, listening to music
Wants to be: a writer for a fashion magazine

PLACES

Aylesbury: a town in England, about one hour from Oxford and London
Aylesbury Grammar and Grange School: two schools for boys and girls from 11 to 18 years old
New Look: a clothes shop in the High Street; there are lots of other shops in the High Street too
MegaSounds: a small music shop in the High Street

Date With

Chapter 1 The New Boy

'The pictures on your locker are cool. Are you a music fan?' Kate looked up. It was the good-looking new boy from Year 9.

Kate was embarrassed. Was her face red? She smiled and hoped there was no food between her teeth from lunch. Then she said, 'Yes, I love music. I want to be a singer one day. My name's Kate. What's your name?'

'I'm Joe and I'm new here. I want to start a band. I play the guitar. Maybe you can be the singer.'

'Wow!' thought Kate. Joe was gorgeous, with his big smile and brown hair. She started to answer, but …

'Joe!' It was Sally and Melissa, two girls from Year 9. Sally had a CD in her hand. 'Joe, thanks for the CD. Are you coming to French with us?'

The two girls took Joe's arms. Joe looked at Kate and said, 'Here, listen to the new 50 Cent CD. See you!'

Kate took the CD. 'Thanks! Have fun in French!'

Disaster!

***

'Hi Kate!' It was Rachel, Kate's 18-year-old sister. Rachel was a student in Brighton, but this week she was at home on holiday. Kate was 13 and she liked the idea of her sister's life in Brighton. No mum or dad, no homework and lots of exciting student parties – fantastic!

Rachel had some photos from Brighton.

'Look. That's my new boyfriend, Sam,' said Rachel.

'Ooh, he's gorgeous,' said Kate. Kate was very pretty, with long blonde hair and big brown eyes. But she didn't have a boyfriend. For a minute, she wanted to be Rachel. Why did Rachel always have a gorgeous boyfriend, and Kate never had anyone? Then she remembered Joe.

'There's a new boy in Year 9,' she told Rachel. 'His locker's opposite mine. Lovely!'

'What, the locker or the boy?' said Rachel.

'The boy, of course!' said Kate. Her sister was very stupid sometimes. 'His name's Joe.'

***

'Kate! It's homework time!' It was Kate's mum.

'She can't do any homework today, Mum. She's thinking about Gorgeous Joe!' said Rachel.

'Please keep quiet, Rachel. Just leave me alone,' said Kate.

Kate went up to her room and sat at her desk. She looked at her maths homework. It was very difficult.

'Maybe Ian can help,' she thought. Kate sat next to Ian in maths this year, and he helped her with the difficult questions. Last week he gave her his mobile number. 'Phone me. We can do our homework together one day,' he said. Ian was nice, and good-looking too. She liked him a lot – but then she started thinking about Joe again …

***

Next day, Kate had a singing lesson at lunchtime and she didn't see Joe or Ian. At the end of the day, she walked to the bus stop with her friends. Suddenly, she remembered something.

'Oh no! My books for tonight's homework are still in my locker. I'm going back for them. See you tomorrow.'

She ran into the school and got her books. Then she saw Joe alone in a classroom. She went in.

'Joe! What are you doing here?' asked Kate.

'I've got detention,' said Joe.

'Oh no, what did you do?' Kate hated detentions.

'Well, I went to Oxford with some friends last night. We saw the Red Hot Chili Peppers there and I came home late. This morning I was tired. In English, I closed my eyes just for a minute, and the teacher saw me. He was very angry.'

Kate loved the Red Hot Chili Peppers.

'You're lucky!' said Kate. 'I wanted to go, but tickets were very expensive …'

'I work at a music shop, MegaSounds, on Saturdays. Someone at the shop gave me tickets,' said Joe. 'Lots of good bands come to

Oxford. Next time, do you want to come too?'

'OK,' said Kate. 'Here's my mobile number. Text me.'

Joe smiled. 'Cool.' Then he looked at the clock. 'Oh no, it's ten past four already. I have to write 'I must not sleep in class' 300 times before five o'clock.'

Kate laughed. 'OK, see you tomorrow. And don't close your eyes again!'

Chapter 2 Boys, boys, boys ...

It was Friday lunchtime. Kate usually had her lunch in the school café with her friends. Between her classroom and the café was the football field. On her way to the café, she saw Joe on the field. She wasn't usually a football fan, but today she watched. Joe looked great in his blue and white football clothes.

'My life is boring now,' thought Kate. 'But maybe I can be Joe's girlfriend and the singer in his band. Then I can have an exciting life.'

'Hey, Kate! You don't often watch football.' It was Ian. He was in the same team as Joe. 'What do you think of the team?' he asked. 'Are we going to be better than Grange School this year?'

Some of the boys stopped and looked at Kate. Joe saw her too. She was very embarrassed. She didn't know anything about football – all her friends knew that.

'Oh, I – er – I'm late for a singing lesson! Bye!' Kate said.

'But it's Friday! You have your singing lesson after maths on Thursday!' said Ian.

'It's different this week. See you!' Kate said. Was her face red?

'That was terrible!' she thought. 'Does Joe think I'm stupid now?'

***

The next morning was Saturday. Kate was in bed. On Saturdays, she had breakfast in bed and read her favourite magazine, GOSSIP. She loved reading about rich and famous people and their exciting lives. 'One day I'm going to be famous too,' she thought.

Her mobile buzzed.

'Maybe it's Joe!'

Kate looked at the phone. It was Ian. 'Why doesn't Joe call?' she thought.

'Hi, Kate! How are you?' said Ian. 'Do you want to come to my house this afternoon? We can do that maths homework together.'

A Saturday afternoon of maths! That wasn't very exciting. But their teacher wanted the homework on Monday morning.

'Yeah, OK,' said Kate. 'About four o'clock?'

'Great!' said Ian. He gave her his address. 'See you at four.'

'Hmmm,' thought Kate. 'Ian's not very cool, but he is a good friend. And I don't know very much about Joe. Is he a nice person, or is he just cool?'

She got some paper and started to write. Which boy did she like best, Ian or Joe?

Her sister came in.

'What's this? A letter?' she said.

Kate said, 'Don't read it! It's nothing!'

'OK, OK!' said Rachel. 'I'm going to buy some new clothes. Do you want to come?'

Kate liked shopping with Rachel. Then she had an idea. 'I want to buy some new music. Can we go to MegaSounds?' she asked.

'But we always go to HMV for CDs,' said Rachel. 'Why do you want to go to MegaSounds? Is that gorgeous new boy going to be there?'

'No,' Kate said. Well, that wasn't true. But how did her sister always know everything? And anyway, maybe Joe wasn't there today. Maybe he didn't work *every* Saturday.

Chapter 3 I'm going to sell my sister!

'Do you like this T-shirt?' asked Rachel.

Rachel and Kate were at New Look in the High Street. There were a lot of clothes shops in Aylesbury, but New Look was Kate and Rachel's favourite shop.

'Yes, it's nice … But when are we going to the music shop?' asked Kate.

'Keep your hair on! The shops close at five-thirty. We've still got two hours,' said Rachel.

'Yeah, but I'm going to Ian's house at four,' said Kate.

'OK, OK. Go to the music shop. But I'm going to buy this T-shirt first. We can meet at MegaSounds,' said Rachel.

***

At MegaSounds, Kate found Joe with lots of Maroon 5 CDs in his arms. He saw her and smiled.

'Hi Kate! This is a surprise!' he said.

'Oh, hi Joe,' said Kate. 'I'm looking for the new Kelis CD.'

'Cool. She's got a great voice.' He put down the CDs in his arms and found a different one. 'Here it is,' said Joe. He gave the CD to Kate.

'What do I say now?' thought Kate. 'Do I ask about tickets for bands in Oxford?'

'Kate!'

It was Rachel. She had a CD in her hand.

'It's your favourite

band! Clive and the Cowboys!'

Kate and Joe looked at the CD. The singers were about 60 years old.

'Your favourite band?!' said Joe.

Kate was embarrassed. Her face was red.

'I'm going to find some more Clive music for you,' said Rachel. She walked back to the worst CDs in the shop.

'Is that your sister? She's funny,' said Joe.

Kate didn't agree. Rachel wasn't funny – she was stupid. 'I'm going to sell my sister one day!' she thought.

'Kate, I'm going to a party at Grange School tonight. Do you want to come? Clive and the Cowboys aren't going to be there, but some good DJs are playing at it.' Joe smiled at Kate. He had a gorgeous smile and beautiful big brown eyes.

'Great!' said Kate. 'And please don't listen to my sister. I'm not a big fan of Clive and the Cowboys.'

'It's OK – I didn't believe her,' said Joe. 'Anyway, a friend gave me some tickets and ...'

'I'm out of here.' It was Rachel. Again. 'I want to look for a skirt in the same colour as my new T-shirt. Don't forget your maths lesson at four o'clock!'

Kate and Joe both looked at their watches. Oh no! It was ten to four already. But Kate didn't want to go. She wanted to ask Joe more about the party. Was this a date? Or did Joe have tickets for lots of friends?

'Maths on a Saturday?' Joe said. 'Oh well, don't be late. See you at the party, maybe.'

Sadly, Kate left the shop.

Her mobile buzzed. It was a message from Ian.

'WHERE R U? I'VE GOT A SURPRISE 4 U'

'A surprise for me!' thought Kate. 'Something nice, I hope.'

Chapter 4

Spots + Messages + Maths Homework = HELP!

Kate walked to Ian's house. Ian opened the door.

His mum was in the kitchen. 'It's nice to meet you, Kate,' she said.

Ian and Kate sat at the table in the dining room. Kate opened her bag. There was a message on her mobile.

It was her sister.

'HOW'S THE DATE WITH MR MATHS?'

'Arrgh!' thought Kate. 'Rachel never stops! Ian and I aren't dating, and Rachel knows that.' Kate quickly put her phone back in her bag.

***

Ian was busy with the homework. He looked up at Kate and smiled. His eyes were lovely – blue, like his jeans.

'Wake up, Kate! Homework time!' he said.

'OK, but first tell me. What's the surprise?' asked Kate.

'No, I'm not going to tell you yet. Finish the homework first!' said Ian.

'Oh, tell me now! Please!' said Kate.

'OK, OK! Well, you know that new film with Orlando Bloom?' said Ian.

'Yes,' said Kate. She loved Orlando Bloom.

'The film's on at the Odeon, tonight at 6.30. I've got two tickets, so we can go together.'

'Great!' Kate smiled at Ian.

Ian was very happy. 'Fantastic! It's a date!'

Kate's smile disappeared. Maybe this wasn't a good idea. Did Ian want to be her boyfriend? What about Joe and the party tonight?

'I can't think about this now,' she thought. 'OK then, Ian,' she said. 'Let's do this homework.'

***

It was five o'clock. There was still a lot of homework.

'I can't think about maths,' thought Kate. 'I need to think about tonight. I'm going to the cinema with Ian but Joe's got a ticket for me for the party too! What am I going to do?'

Kate went to the bathroom. In the mirror, she saw a big spot on her nose.

'Oh no! Joe isn't going to want a girlfriend with a spot!' she thought. 'What can I do?! Maybe Ian has something for spots.' She looked around the bathroom, but she didn't find anything. Then she remembered – her sister sometimes used toothpaste for spots! She put some toothpaste on her nose.

In the dining room, Kate sat down quickly. She looked at her books. Ian didn't see her nose.

'There's a message on your mobile again,' said Ian.

'Oh, is there?' Kate quickly got her mobile out of her bag.

'MEET AT THE PARTY AT 8? IT'S GOING 2 B FUN.'

It was Joe. Kate was embarrassed. Did Ian see the message? She wanted to answer Joe's text – but she was next to Ian!

'Ian, sorry. I need to go to the bathroom again!'

Ian looked up. 'Are you OK, Kate? What's that on your nose?'

'Yeah, I'm OK! And my nose is OK too!' Kate ran to the bathroom. She closed the door and wrote a text to Joe.

'C U AT GRANGE SCHOOL AT 8.'

She pressed 'send'. But nothing happened! 'Oh no!' thought Kate. 'No credit! My mobile needs more credit, and I didn't buy any in town. What can I do now? I can't send a message to Joe on Ian's phone! But is Joe going to be at the party tonight anyway? Or is he going to wait at home for an answer from me?'

***

'Ian, I must go!' Kate ran into the dining room.

'But there's still lots of homework … and we can walk to the cinema together from here,' said Ian.

'I need to buy some new clothes!' said Kate.

'Keep your hair on! You don't need new clothes for the cinema. You look great now,' said Ian.

Kate thought quickly. She said, 'My sister's going back to Brighton tonight. The clothes are for her. I must go! See you!'

Ian sat in the dining room. He was very surprised. Was something wrong with Kate today?

Chapter 5 Mobile mistake

Kate went up to her bedroom. She wanted to think. 'I need to text Joe, but I don't have any credit for my mobile. What can I do?' Then she had an idea.

Rachel's bedroom was empty. Rachel was in the bathroom. Kate wrote to Joe on her sister's mobile.

'THIS IS MY SISTER'S PHONE. NO CREDIT ON MINE. C U AT GRANGE SCHOOL PARTY AT 8. KATE XX'

Then she wrote Joe's number on Rachel's phone.

'What are you doing? That's my phone!' It was Rachel.

Rachel took her phone and read the message. 'You're writing love messages on my phone!' she said angrily.

'I'm sorry, but I can't use my phone. I haven't got any credit,' said Kate. 'Please can I send the message?'

'No! Don't take my things!' said Rachel.

'Rachel, please! This message is important!' said Kate.

Rachel was still angry, but she gave the phone to Kate. Kate quickly pressed 'send'.

'Next time, ask me first,' said Rachel.

After two minutes, Rachel came into Kate's room. 'There's a message for you on my phone,' she said.

Kate took the phone. It was a text from Ian.

'WHAT, NO CINEMA? BUT A PARTY IS OK 2. IAN XX'

'Oh no! I sent the message about the party to Ian,

not to Joe!' Kate looked at the address book on her phone. Ian's number was next to Joe's.

'What am I going to do now? I can't go on a date with Joe and Ian to the same party!'

'Rachel, can I send another text?' asked Kate.

'Is it very important?' asked Rachel.

'Yes!' said Kate.

'OK,' said Rachel.

Kate sent a text to Ian.

'GOT A HEADACHE. STAYING AT HOME. SORRY. KATE XX'

Then she wrote to Joe.

'C U AT GRANGE SCHOOL PARTY AT 8.'

This time, she wrote Joe's number very carefully. Then she pressed 'send' and gave the phone back to her sister.

***

It was quarter to eight. Kate dressed in her favourite clothes and looked in the mirror. 'Oh no! What can I do about that terrible spot on my nose?!' she thought. But there was no time. She ran to the door.

'I'm meeting a friend from school! Bye!' said Kate to her mum and dad. They were in the living room. They always watched a film on TV on Saturday nights.

'OK! Be home before 10!' they said. Kate was lucky. Her family lived in the centre of town. It was an easy walk to the shops and cafés ... and to Grange School.

Kate walked down the street to the party. 'Is Ian going to be angry with me?' she thought. 'I hope not. He doesn't need to know about my date with Joe.'

She was happy. 'Tonight's going to be fun,' she thought.

***

Kate was on the street in front of Grange School. She looked at her watch. '8.05,' she thought. 'So where's Joe?'

She looked across the street to the school door. Then she stopped.

Ian and Joe were both there!

'Oh no!' Kate went behind a tree. 'What are they doing? Why is Ian here? Does Ian know about my date with Joe? Ian mustn't see me! My text message to him said, 'Got a headache – staying at home.' What can I do?'

There was only one answer. She went home. 'This is a disaster,' she thought. 'What can I say to Ian and Joe?'

Chapter 6 Date With disaster!

'Kate, eat your breakfast. It's going to be cold soon!' said Kate's dad. Usually Kate loved her dad's big Sunday breakfast, but today she wasn't hungry.

'Poor Kate's tired! She had two dates last night!' said Rachel.

'Is that true, Kate?' asked their mum.

'It's not true! I don't have a boyfriend!' Kate said. She ran up to her room.

Soon there was someone at her bedroom door.

'It's me – Rachel. Are you OK, Kate?' she asked.

Kate told her sister everything.

'Kate, it's OK. Ian and Joe are your friends,' said Rachel.

'Maybe,' said Kate. 'I just don't know …'

***

Kate went back to the kitchen. She heard the phone. Was it Joe or Ian? Kate didn't want to answer it.

'Hi Kate! How are you feeling?' It was Ian.

'I'm better today, thanks. And Ian, I'm very sorry about last night.'

'That's OK,' said Ian. 'I didn't see your second message at home. My mobile was in my bag and I didn't hear it. I went to Grange School and waited for you. You didn't come, so then I looked at my messages. But I met Joe at the school – you know, the new boy in Year 9, the one in my football team. Well, he had some tickets so I went to the party anyway. It was fun. I changed the tickets for the cinema. Do you want to see the film tonight? It starts at six.'

'OK, great!' said Kate. 'Let's meet at the cinema.'

They said goodbye. Kate put down the phone and thought, 'Ian isn't angry about last night, so Joe didn't talk to Ian about me. Maybe *this* date isn't going to be a disaster!'

***

'That was a great film,' said Kate. She and Ian walked out of the cinema together.

'Yes, it was good,' said Ian. 'I'm hungry now. Let's get some food.'

There was a café near the cinema. People often went there after a film. They started to walk to it.

Suddenly, Ian pointed to someone. 'Look, Kate, it's Joe!'

'OH NO!' thought Kate. 'I'm here with Ian! What's Joe going to think? I can't run away! Is this a date with disaster again?!'

It was too late. 'Joe!' shouted Ian. Joe looked up and crossed the road. Then Kate saw a girl behind Joe.

'Ian, who's that girl?' she asked.

'It's Joe's girlfriend, Laura. I met her last night at the party,' said Ian.

Kate was angry for a minute. Then she was embarrassed. 'So Joe didn't ask me on a date to the party!' she thought. 'It was just a night out with some friends! I'm so stupid.'

Joe was in front of them now. He smiled and said, 'Hi again, Kate. I met Ian at the party last night. Why weren't you there too?'

Kate was embarrassed. 'I had a headache.'

Then Joe said, 'Kate, this is my girlfriend, Laura. She goes to my old school in Oxford.'

'Hi,' said Kate. Was her face red? She still liked Joe, and she wasn't very happy about Laura. 'Are you going to be in Joe's band?'

'Laura plays the drums. She's fantastic,' Joe said. He smiled at Laura.

'Luckily Oxford's not very far away. I can come and play in the band here every weekend,' said Laura.

'But we still need a good singer,' said Joe. 'Kate?'

'But –' Kate didn't know. Laura had a nice smile, like Joe. 'But three isn't always a good number,' she thought. 'Can we all be friends in a band together?'

'Well, think about it,' said Joe. 'We're going to have auditions next week.'

'I can play the guitar,' said Ian suddenly. 'Can I come to the auditions too?'

Kate was surprised. She knew Ian was good at maths. But the guitar too?

Joe smiled. 'That's great, Ian. So we've got Kate the singer, Laura on the drums, Ian and me on guitar – we've got a band already! When are we going to be on MTV?!'

They all laughed.

Kate was happy now. 'I feel very lucky,' she thought. 'Joe and Ian are still my friends, and maybe I can be in a fantastic band! I don't need to be Joe's girlfriend. Friends are more important than boyfriends anyway.'

Joe and Laura went into the café. Ian waited for Kate at the café door.

'Come on, Kate! You're always dreaming!' Ian smiled.

Kate thought, 'I want to know more about Ian. He's different from Joe, but maybe he's cool too. Maybe I *can* have a boyfriend with a guitar ...'

She followed her friends into the café. 'Let's talk music!' she said.

FIRST DATE

Where do British teenagers go for their first date? We asked some teenagers in London.

Carly, 14 'On my first date, I went to the cinema. It's a great place for a first date, because you can talk about the film at the end!'

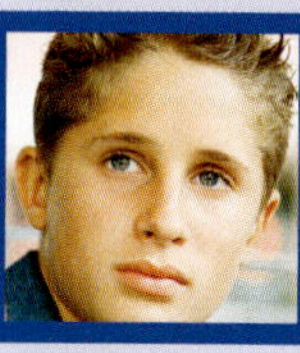

Paul, 12 'The best thing for a first date? A football match. My favourite team is Arsenal. I want an Arsenal fan as a girlfriend, so we can go to matches together.'

Jenny, 14 'I'd like a first date in a restaurant. Pizza's my favourite food. A restaurant is a good place because you can talk a lot. You can't talk in a cinema!'

Sam, 13 'I went to the funfair for my first date with my girlfriend. We went on lots of different rides and laughed a lot.'

Where do people in your country go for their first date?

Find these words in the pictures:

funfair match ride pizza

I was SO embarrassed!

It's your first date. You want to have a fantastic time, but sometimes plans go wrong ...

'I had a date with a boy from my class. He asked me to the cinema. It was our first date. At the cinema, I waited and waited. It started to rain. Then he called me on my mobile. "Where are you? The film starts in two minutes!" he said. I was at the wrong cinema!' **Laura, 12**

'I was at a friend's party and my new girlfriend, Anna, was with me. There was some cool music and I started to dance in the centre of the room. I did some breakdancing. Everyone watched. Suddenly, my shoe came off my foot and hit Anna on the nose! It was terrible!' **Joel, 13**

'On my first date, I went shopping with my boyfriend, Jake. We walked around the shopping centre and had a burger. Everything was cool. We saw one of my friends and I talked to her for a few minutes. Jake didn't stay with us. My friend went, and I saw Jake at the jewellery shop window. "That's nice," I thought. "He's buying me something." I walked to the window and put my arms around him. But it wasn't Jake! I didn't know this boy at all! Jake was in a shop opposite the jewellery shop and he saw everything. He laughed, but I was very embarrassed!' **Molly, 13**

Which of these first date disasters is the worst?

Find these words in the pictures:

breakdancing jewellery

Are you a dating

Do you have dating disasters like Kate? Or are you good at the dating game? Answer the questions and find out.

1 There's a new boy/girl in your class. You like him/her a lot. What do you say?

☐ **a.** 'Hello, my name's … . What are your hobbies?'

☐ **b.** 'Hi. You're the best-looking person in our class. Come out with me on Saturday.'

☐ **c.** Nothing. You're too embarrassed.

2 You're on the bus. A gorgeous boy/girl phones you on your mobile. What do you do?

☐ **a.** Have a short conversation and plan to meet at the weekend.

☐ **b.** Talk loudly for an hour on the bus. Some people on the bus look at you angrily. You don't care – this is true love!

☐ **c.** Plan a conversation in your head, then answer. But it's too late. The person at the other end didn't wait.

3 It's your first date, and you like this boy/girl a lot. Five minutes before the date, he/she phones you and says, 'I'm sorry. I'm going to be late.' What do you do?

☐ **a.** Ask, 'Are you very busy? Do you want to meet on a different day?'

☐ **b.** Feel angry and say, 'I don't wait for anyone! Enjoy your next date – with a new boy/girlfriend!'

☐ **c.** Say nothing and start to cry.

disaster?

4 You're meeting your new boy/girlfriend for a pizza. What do you wear?

- ☐ **a.** Your favourite jeans and a cool T-shirt.
- ☐ **b.** Expensive new clothes. You look like Orlando Bloom/Keira Knightley at the Oscars.
- ☐ **c.** You can't decide. In the end, you wear the same things as yesterday. They're a bit dirty, but who cares?

5 You've got a date. At home, your parents ask, 'Are you going to meet your new boy/girlfriend?' What do you say?

- ☐ **a.** 'I'm meeting someone from school. He/she's nice, but we're just friends.' You don't feel embarrassed.
- ☐ **b.** 'Yes, I'm meeting (name) and he/she's the love of my life!'
- ☐ **c.** 'I'm not meeting anyone. I'm just taking the dog for a walk.' You feel very embarrassed.

Which answer did you give most?

a. Fantastic! You're very good at the dating game. You make friends with a boy/girl first and think about love second.

b. You love dreaming about love, but sometimes this isn't a good idea. Life isn't always like a dream. Try to think about boys/girls as friends too.

c. Maybe you like someone a lot. But is it difficult to talk to him/her? Many people have the same trouble. Can you go out with him/her with a group of your friends? Sometimes this is easier than a date for two.

FACT FILE

MOBILE

Text messages are cheap, quick and easy! With a text, you can:

- say a quick hello
- send pictures and funny stories
- plan a day out with your friends

And it's fun too. Use these abbreviations and write the best texts in town!

What do the abbreviations mean? For some help, look below.

see you later | wait for me | thank you | are you OK?
bye for now | I like you | as soon as possible | I love you

MAD

DID YOU KNOW?

▸▸ In the UK, teenagers send over 1 billion text messages every month. That's more than 30 million texts a day!

▸▸ What do 70% of American teenagers want for Christmas? Mobile phones!

▸▸ In the UK, 90% of people from 11 to 16 years old have mobile phones. 10% of them talk on their mobiles for more than 45 minutes a day.

Are you mobile mad? Answer the questions and find out.

a) Do you always want a smaller mobile phone? Yes / No

b) Your friend's got a new mobile. He/she can take photos and use the internet with it. Do you want one too? Yes / No

c) You are bored. Do you play a game on your phone? Yes / No

d) You leave your mobile at home. You live 20 minutes away. Do you go home and get your phone? Yes / No

e) Do you use your phone more than five times a day? Yes / No

You get a point for every 'yes' answer.

4 – 5 points: You can't live without your mobile phone!

2 – 3 points: You like having a mobile, but you don't use it all the time.

0 – 1 points: Mobile phones aren't very important to you. You like talking to your friends face to face.

Chapters 1–2

Before you read

1 What is the past simple of these irregular verbs?
a) see **b)** sit **c)** take **d)** tell **e)** think **f)** give **g)** run
h) know **i)** get

2 Which of these adjectives describe:
a) personality **b)** appearance **c)** feelings?
You can use your dictionary.
gorgeous **good-looking** **cool**
pretty **angry** **stupid** **embarrassed**

3 Which of these words isn't something about school? Use your dictionary.
a) detention **b)** homework **c)** classroom **d)** fan
e) locker **f)** lesson **g)** maths

4 Complete the sentences with these verbs.
text **smile** **buzz** **laugh**
a) Did my mobile … ? Oh good, I've got a message.
b) I always … very loudly at funny stories.
c) I've got my mobile, so he can … me his address.
d) … for the camera, please.

After you read

5 Answer the questions.
a) Kate meets Joe at the lockers. Do they talk about:
i) homework ii) music iii) films?
b) How does Kate know Ian?
c) Why does Joe have a detention after school?
d) Does Kate often watch football?
e) Where do Rachel and Kate want to go on Saturday afternoon?

6 What do you think?
a) Would you like a sister like Rachel? Why/Why not?
b) Who is a better boyfriend for Kate, Ian or Joe? Why?

Chapters 3–4

Before you read

7 Answer the questions. You can use your dictionary.

a) Your mobile hasn't got any credit. Can you call someone on it?

b) You have a big spot on your face. Do you feel gorgeous?

c) Which place is better for a date: a bank or a party?

d) You look in a mirror. What can you see?

8 Complete the sentences with these words. You can use your dictionary.

ticket press toothpaste send

a) You can't get on the train without a … .

b) I clean my teeth with white … .

c) I … letters to people in lots of different countries.

d) Oh no! I did my homework on the computer but I didn't … 'save'. Now I can't find it.

After you read

9 Are these sentences true or false? Correct the false sentences.

a) Kate sees Ian at the music shop.

b) Rachel finds a CD for Kate. It's Kate's favourite music.

c) Joe wants to go to the party with Kate on Saturday evening.

d) Ian helps Kate with her English homework.

e) Ian has got tickets for the cinema.

f) Kate puts toothpaste on her nose because she has a spot.

g) Kate can't send a message to Joe because she has no credit on her phone.

h) Kate walks to the cinema with Ian.

10 What do you think?

a) Is Kate going to go to the cinema with Ian? What about the party with Joe?

b) Two people are going to enjoy the evening. One person is not. Who's going to have a bad time: Joe, Ian or Kate?

Chapters 5–6

Before you read

11 Match these words with the correct definitions.

a) Take an aspirin for that ...	**i)** drums.
b) I wanted to be in the film, so I decided to go to the ...	**ii)** disaster.
c) Everything went wrong. It was a ...	**iii)** headache.
d) I love being loud, so I'm learning to play the ...	**iv)** audition.

12 Is Kate going to have a boyfriend at the end of the story? Who?

After you read

13 Kate needs to send a message to Joe. Answer the questions.

a) How does Kate send a text about the party?
b) Why is Rachel angry?
c) Who gets Kate's message about the party?

14 Are these sentences true or false? Correct the false sentences.

a) Kate sent the text about the party to Ian by mistake.
b) Joe and Ian were both at the party.
c) Kate went to the party and danced a lot.
d) The next day, Joe and Kate went to the cinema together.
e) Laura was at the party on Saturday.
f) Ian plays the drums.
g) Kate likes Ian a lot at the end of the story.

15 What do you think?

a) Is Laura lucky? Is Joe a good boyfriend? Why/Why not?
b) What's going to happen to Kate, Ian, Laura and Joe? Think about:
i) their love life **ii)** Joe's band